SOPHISTICATED
ALLIGATORS

VILLARD

NEW YORK

1995

SOPHISTICATED ALLIGATORS

Noël Clark Miller

Copyright © 1995 by Noël Miller

All rights reserved under International and Pan-American
Copyright Conventions. Published in the United States by
Villard Books, a division of Random House, Inc., New York, and simultaneously
in Canada by Random House of Canada Limited, Toronto.

Villard Books is a registered trademark of Random House, Inc.

Library of Congress Cataloging–in–Publication Data
Miller, Noël.
Sophisticated alligators/Noël Miller.
p.   cm.
ISBN 0-679-44321-5
1. Statesmen—Caricatures and cartoons. 2. Kings and rulers—
Caricatures and cartoons. 3. Celebrities—Caricatures and cartoons.
4. Alligators—Humor. 5. Characters and characteristics—
Humor. I. Title
D107.M55   1995
920'.00207—dc20   95-247

Noël Miller's *Sophisticated Alligators* would like to express
their appreciation for the good work done by the Louisiana
chapter of The Nature Conservancy. The Nature Conservancy is dedicated
to the protection of habitats for rare and endangered animals,
plants, and natural communities, including that of the alligator.

Manufactured in Italy
9   8   7   6   5   4   3   2
First Edition
Book design by JoAnne Metsch

TO MY FAMILY, WHO DESERVE NOTHING LESS

▲▼

INTRODUCTION

The alligators that inhabit the following pages (or, as some might put it, infest them) have a history. As human beings, we cherish our personal histories and like to keep them handy to explain ourselves to others of our species. When we speak at luncheons or banquets we prefer to be introduced first, with a brief curriculum vitae. When we're hunting for jobs, we send our résumés to potential employers. Upon meeting new acquaintances, we mention where we are from and solicit the same information. We search for people we might know in common, experiences we might have shared. Alternatively, we pull out all manner of business cards and family photographs to give our new friends a better idea of our place in the world. I would like to perform this service for my alligators—as though I were introducing them as luncheon speakers, without the attendant dangers.

I first came to know them one early spring morning in southwest Louisiana—several years ago now—when I took a houseguest fishing during the gators' mating season. Everything happened at once that spring: we had a forcing warm spell after a long, cold winter. Azaleas and camellias, wisteria, swamp lilies, climbing jasmine, and dogwoods all decided to bloom at the same time, something they rarely do, and probably shouldn't.

Once a year, our family visits this paradisical part of the world to stay in what used to be my grandmother's house. Our timing has been determined by our children's spring vacations. The weather we expect is unpredictable. One memorable year, we had eleven children under the roof and it rained for ten straight days.

The year I'm speaking of, however, we hit the jackpot. For the whole two weeks of our holiday, we experienced an intensity of spring as powerful as anything I've known. The snowy egrets, with their exquisite spring plumage, were busier than we've ever seen them; courting, nesting, and hatching, so it seemed, all at once. I've heard that, after we left, everything just plain gave out. The blossoms dropped off all the bushes and vines, and that was that. During our visit though, as I've said, every flower that could possibly bloom was doing it. Also (though I don't suppose they have much interest in horticulture) I've never seen a bunch of alligators so excited.

Quite a few alligators inhabit the pond where we fish. One old dowager in particular returns to the same stretch of shore every spring, like a club woman who has staked out her family cabana in East Hampton. They aren't usually what I'd call animated: the ability to tell the difference between a floating log and an alligator is something that's acquired with practice and patience.

On the morning in question, however, as my friend and I

pushed sleepily off from shore in a rowboat, the peaceful pond was transformed. Rutting alligators made an incredible racket in the dark around us. Every now and then a couple of tails would flip up somewhere near us, as the creatures gamboled and (I guess) groped, under the water. Their actual couplings, we surmised, took place in the privacy of the bulrushes.*

The houseguest was a gentleman of the old school: the imperturbable, pipe-smoking sort. Fishing was out of the question, but, if he minded this at all, he had better manners than to say so to his hostess. He and I drifted gently around the pond, enjoying all the commotion. As alligator bulls hissed and snorted and grunted around us (occasionally nudging our boat in their enthusiasm), he chatted charmingly away about one of his many interests: Meissen porcelain.

After our fishless return to the house, I wrote the verse about Lou. Lou was closely followed by Alexander, and, ever since then, alligators have been obtruding themselves upon me, preoccupied, almost always, by food and sex. Entertainment is also important to these picturesque creatures. They seek it and, with cheerful reptilian virtuosity, often offer it at the theater—which, of course, they pronounce "thee-ay-ter," to rhyme with themselves.

I entertain prestidigitators, slick operators, real estate salesmen, and waiters—the roster of occupations is almost endless. I see them

*We were wrong. I have since learned that they always mate in the water.

stepping out of elevators, beeping their electronic calculators, having the devil's own time of it on department store escalators. And guzzling candied sweet potaters, their favorite food. No matter how we spell it, this (to them) delectable dish will, in the following pages, always rhyme with *alligator.* So, as I've said, will *theater.*

The word *alligator* is remarkably beautiful. It's a supple word, as it should be, and versatile about the company it keeps. It can go along happily with either *legislator* or *literate whore.* The sound of it is as euphonious as *cellar door,* with which, in a pinch, it can be made to rhyme. (Poor Aida discovers this, to her dismay, after her famous aria "Ritorna, alligatòr.")

My first encounter with these beasts—specifically, with Lou and Alexander—took place a number of years ago. Since then I have had to adjust to being haunted by alligators. Let my readers beware: the same thing may happen to you. You, too, may wake up at four in the morning with shouts of "Alma mater!" "Violate her!" "Carburetor!" "Decapitator! (Ode to Mme. Guillotine)," and so forth. There have been periods of rebellion—not only mine but those of my long-suffering family.

There are compensations, of course, although offhand I can't think of many. This alligator obsession is threatening the other writing I do. A perfectly nice comic novel is in danger of being dragged down altogether. The characters have all developed voracious appetites, and one of them has just insulted another by calling her a "blue-eyed alligator." I find myself describing one old man, increasingly often, as having a green complexion: he will die, of a surfeit of absinthe, in my next chapter. None of these is a good sign.

In one way, and one way only, these animals may broaden my horizons. All of my alligators *(Alligator mississippiensis)* hail from our American South. They do, however, have cousins in China *(Alligator sinensis)*. These are smaller and rarer, with longer noses and somewhat different complexions. It would be fun, one day, to go over and see them. No doubt they conform to the culture around them, and respect the aged—the longer I put off my visit, the better it's likely to be. I can see myself now, as an old, old woman, floating in the shallows of the Yangtze spitting fish scales, revered for my great age and for my eccentricity, while my fellow tourists explore the Great Wall and similar cultural monuments. I might try the same thing along the Atchafalaya, but I'd merely blend in with the surrounding scenery, to be pointed out by passing swamp tour operators in their airboats.

My chief reason for wishing to publish this small book is to spread the alligator contagion. Misery loves company, and the idea of other people thrashing about and muttering into their pillows is profoundly comforting. I hope, too, that my readers will find pleasure in this exercise—as I have. That said, we should bring on the alligators. The introductory speech has gone on long enough, and the master of ceremonies is showing his teeth. It is time for the banquet to begin!

SOPHISTICATED
ALLIGATORS

S. A.

Sophisticated Alligators,
When they wish to celebrate a
Small occasion, or a greater,
Take a box at the theater.

NYMPHOMANIA

Once an alligator satyr
Sprang upon a nymph, to mate her.
This seemed wildly to elate her:
"Wow!" cried she—"Half goat, half gator!"

SWEET PRINCE

"To be, or not to be, an alligator?"
Thus queried sweet Prince Hamlet, vacillator.
"To suffer, or to take arms: which is greater?"
His father's ghost, irate and then irater,
Lost patience with the young procrastinator.
"Revenge," it cried, "on my assassinator!
Slay me that fratricidal infiltrator!
Slaughter, I say, the vile adulterator—
But, Hamlet, leave to heav'n your faithless mater."

Impelled by this paternal exhortation
To action, Hamlet had an inspiration:
"The play's the thing! I'll catch, while a spectator,
The conscience of this regicidal satyr!"
Thus Hamlet plotted, to confound his foe,
An evening of miching mallecho.
Himself directing, princely orchestrator,
He lured the king and queen to the theater,
Murder most foul and strange to re-create there.

Eight characters, thereafter, found quietus
With daggers, spears, and other apparatus,
With poisoned wine, and mad, melodious drowning.
The trembling survivors, shocked and frowning,
Told how Prince Hamlet shouted: "Die, thou traitor!
Incestuous, murderous damnèd alligator!"
And, dying, pierced with poison Claudius's breast.
Thus Hamlet carried out the ghost's behest.
May flights of angels sing him to his rest!

DUCHESS

Edward Windsor, alligator,
Vapid British abdicator,
Lost his crown and, instead, got a
Crocodile inamorata.
Offered marriage morganatic,
This chic temptress democratic
Replied, "Bert, not on your life!
'Mrs. Edward Eighth, housewife?'
Not 'Queen Wallis'? Inasmuch as
That's not on, I'll be a duchess."
So, for love and love alone,
Edward Eighth gave up his throne.
That's how George and Mary's slim son
Married Wallis Warfield Simpson.

HUMBERT

Humbert Humbert, alligator,
Erudite but aging satyr,
Loved Lolita, nymphet nubile.
Lust his glasses would bedew while
Licking her old tennis shoe! Vile
Longings swayed him: to palpate her,
Intimately titillate her,
Ultimately penetrate her.
Failing, though, to stimulate her,
Humbert, in frustration, ate her.

SHREDDERS

Witness Fawn and Ollie, gators,
Patriotic masticators
Watch administrative folly
Shredded fine by Fawn and Ollie.

SALOME

Once Salome, alligator,
Saucy, seven-veiled gyrator,
Made King Herod shout, "Fantastic!"
With her dance ecdysiastic,
Supple limbs and joints elastic.

Herod, moved to jubilation
By Salome's undulation,
Let her, as she came unwrappedest,
Claim the head of John the Baptist.

LIZZIE

Lizzie Borden, alligator,
Took an ax and gave her mater
Forty whacks.

When she'd done, she gave her pater
(Who dropped by a moment later)
Forty-one.

Thus did Lizzie Borden, gator,
Give her folks her imprimatur.

DON JUAN

Don Giovanni, alligator,
Eager Spanish fornicator,
Thought the world was a bordello
Cataloged by Leporello.

THE PASSIONATE GATOR TO HIS LOVE

Come live with me and be my alligator,
And we will all the pleasures, soon and later,
Sample that pond and bayou, slime congealed
And all the snake-infested swamp can yield.

There we will lie, entwined among the bogs,
Concealed from all, impersonating logs,
Or, ambulating gently when night falls,
We'll roar our alligator madrigals.

There when we sun together on the rocks
I'll make thee pretty alligator socks.
Iris and lilies shall festoon thy head
And armadillos, living or quite dead.

There I will make thee up a bed of roses
With frogs and lizards leaping through the posies.
Be in these pleasures my collaborator,
Move in with me and be my alligator.

THE NYMPH'S REPLY TO THE GATOR

If the world and love were young,
And truth in any reptile's tongue,
These verses might persuade me, soon or later,
To live with you and be your alligator.

NIXON

Richard Nixon, alligator,
Eighteen-minute expurgator!
Stonewalling prevaricator,
Unindicted Watergater:
One and only, then or later,
Pardoned coconspiragator.

GREEN THUMB

Gertrude Jekyll, alligator,
Landscaped many a fine estate. Her
Lovely gardens, now antique,
Are still great spots for hide and seek,
Whose blooms, while English tongues can speak'll
Praise the name of Gertrude Jekyll.

CLEOPATRA

Cleopatra Alligator
With Great Caesar, Imperator,
Barged in splendor on the Nile,
Snooting every crocodile.

TURNCOAT

Benedict Arnold Alligator,
Slippery, falsely smiling traitor,
Telling his troops, "I'll see ya later!"
Scrammed, with a British navigator.

LAWYER

Habeas Corpus Alligator,
Agile courtroom litigator,
Mouths false allegations vile
With a crocodilian smile.

MONA

Mona Lisa Alligator,
Enigmatic contemplator,
Smiling, "Dolce far niente,"
Dreams of pasta, cooked al dente.

BEC FIN

Gaston the Gourmet, a slick masticator,
Squired Blanche to a bistro to gladden and sate her.
"Garçon!" he admonished their trembling waiter:
"Hors d'oeuvres à la carte, then we'll dine à la gator."

HEAVYWEIGHT

Hail Muhammad Ali, gator,
As "The Greatest, not "The Greator."
He, with boxing's fastest lip,
Twice won the world's championship.

ROSTROPOVICH

Rostropovich, alligator,
Soloist and orchestrator,
Uses elbows, knees, and eyebrows
To enchant plain folks and highbrows,
Making music sweet and mellow
While conducting from the cello.

OTIS

Skunk sandwiches, fresh or decayed, are
What young Otis Alligator
Eats while he's at the job he's paid for:
Elevator operator.

ROMAN MATRON

Lucia Flavia, alligator,
Built a little incubator.
This her children, somewhat later,
Filially addressed as "Mater."

JACK THE RIPPER

Jack the Ripper, alligator,
Lunatic eviscerator,
Stalked his prey through London fog
Masquerading as a log.

VENUS DE MILO

Goddess! Glorious alligator!
What archaic depredator,
Seeking beauty to deface,
Robbed us of your kind embrace?
Now all lovers, meek and mighty,
Worship armless Aphrodite.

Noël

PALETTE TO PALATE

Beatrix Potter, alligator,
Fabulist and illustrator,
Drew with care her charming creatures'
Furry forms and pleasing features.
All correctly shod and hatted,
Collared, flounced, and/or cravated.
Beatrix labored to create them
True to life as she could make them,
Until teatime, when she ate them.
This is what may happen when you
Limn an alligator's menu.

SONNET FROM SHAKESPEARE

Unhappy reptile! With despairing cries,
Hunted for handbags, I lament my state
And mourn for all the lively things I ate
Till tears pour from my alligator eyes.
Outcast and lonely, quite beyond all hope
Of company or friendship—so depressed!
I wish my appetites had smaller scope:
I've eaten all the friends I once possessed,
Or driven them away. Myself despising,
I lift my head and bellow, desperate.
Thine answer, sweet as any lark's, surprising,
Thrills and redeems me. Dear, let's celebrate!
With thy sweet love, remembered from last spring,
I'll crown myself an alligator king!

ABRAHAM LINCOLN

Hail Abe Lincoln, Alligator,
As the Great Emancipator!
Back in eighteen fifty-eight, our
Fledgling backwoods legislator
Made his name as a debater
Battling Illinois's Senator
Douglas ("Little Giant"), orator.
Abe lost then but, two years later,
Presidential candidate, o'er-
Whelmed the whole electorate! Four
Tough years we inaugurate. War
Split the land. Might any state for
Its own self now legislate? Or,
Joined with others, abdicate? More,
Style themselves Confederate? Or,
Once united, separate? Or,
Should the Union dominate, or
What? Not to equivocate, nor

Strain our *e pluribus unum,*
Abe won the war and saved the Union.

The Union thus inviolate, her
Steadfast old administrator
(Healer, not exacerbator)
Spoke of reconciliation
At his next inauguration.

Alas! Honest Alligator!
Abraham, the Liberator,
Felled by an assassinator,
Lost his life at Ford's Theatre.

THE GATORS MEET MISS MANNERS

Smile for Miss Manners! Tell her: "Hi!
Arbiter elegantiae!"
Gators, greet this famous writer.
Emulate, but do not bite her.

A social structure quite complex
Governs these reptiles picturesque:
Omnivorous feeders, fertile breeders
Not unlike her Gentle Readers';
While problems similar perplex
Them: territory, food, and sex.

Their eating habits may appall
The faint of heart; but, all in all,
Are eminently practical.

A gator cruel may grossly drool
While lunching on a gallinule.
She's merely crunching it to gruel
To feed her young ones, minuscule.
Enthusiastic eaters, they
Enjoy their birds ground up this way.

If she'll teach them the Golden Rule,
We'll found an Alligator School
And title her, like a dictator,
Alligator Arbitrator.

LINDBERGH

Charles A. Lindbergh, alligator,
Pioneering aviator,
Stands beside the plane he flew—his
Trusty *Spirit of St. Louis.*

ARTS AND CRAFTS

William Morris, alligator,
Writer, craftsman, decorator,
Painter, scribe, illuminator,
Visionary ruminator,
Formed, with workman's hands and poet's heart,
Beautiful and useful works of art.

ADAM AND EVE

Adam and Eve, alligators,
Injudicious propagators,
Lost their Eden to placate a
Serpentine insinuator.

WHISTLER'S MATER

When James Whistler, alligator,
Made a portrait of his mater
All in black and gray and white,
Ma got mad enough to bite.
"James!" she snapped. "You should have seen,
Gators *must* be painted green!"

MARGARET THATCHER

Margaret Thatcher, alligator:
Careful, don't exasperate her!
Once, as Britain's head of state, her
Voice could silence all debate. Her
Hands the rod of Empire swayed; her
Lightest whim would be obeyed! Where
Is she, now she's past her heyday?
She's still Britain's Iron Lady!

SUNUNU

John Sununu, alligator,
Hedonistic ambulator,
Traveled, heedless of inflation,
Stylishly across the nation.

RIP VAN WINKLE

Rip Van Winkle, alligator,
Hudson Valley hibernator,
Snoozed for twenty years' duration
After an unwise libation.

PRINCESS DI

As wee infants, Britain's princes
Snacked on sugarplums and quinces
Which Diana, gorgeous gator,
Packed in their perambulator.

BORIS YELTSIN

Here's to Boris Yeltsin, gator,
Russia's roguish liberator!
Since he's been elected, Yeltsin
Tells folks they must pull their belts in.

ROMEO AND JULIET

Romeo and Juliet, gators,
Juvenile self-immolators,
Loved with an unruly passion—
Star-crossed, rash, and out of fashion.

CICERO

Marcus Tullius Cicero, gator,
Ancient Rome's renowned orator,
Saddened by her tarnished glories
Cried, *"O tempora! O mores!"*

CICERO

HENRY VIII

Henry Tudor, alligator,
Nuptials abbreviator,
Chose, to spare himself frustration,
Divorce, or decapitation.

ARKANSAS TRAVELERS

Bill's and Hillary's and Chelsea's
Favorite duds are dungarees. These
Alligators, out to please,
Choose outfits that have got no frills
On Chelsea's, Hillary's, or Bill's.

"THE ALLIGATOR"

Rene Lacoste, alligator,
Tennis star and innovator,
Designed his own shirts and jackets,
And the first steel tennis racquets.

OPRAH

Oprah Winfrey, alligator,
Talk show host and commentator,
Talks about life, love, and diet.
Oprah simply can't be quiet.
Oprah Winfrey! Fat or thin, she
Smiles, and isn't ever grinchy.
Till this bad old world is sin free,
Let's tune in to Oprah Winfrey!

MR. UNIVERSE

Alligator action hero!
Smiling, like the youthful Nero,
Arnold Schwarzenegger, gator,
A.k.a. "The Terminator,"
Shows us, with his manly poses,
Veins as thick as fire hoses.

SATCHMO

Louis Armstrong, alligator,
Jazzman and improvisator,
Blew his trumpet, strong and sweet,
From West End to Basin Street.

ALMA MATER

Sarah Porter, alligator,
Premier female educator,
Exemplar and motivator,
Taught her girls to sit up straighter,
So that each, with concentration,
Might absorb indoctrination.
Then each student could comport her
Self exactly like Miss Porter.

BEATLEMANIA

John and George and Paul and Ringo,
With their Liverpudlian lingo,
Sang "I Want to Hold Your Hand."
Then, becoming rather hepper,
They progressed to Sgt Pepper
And his Lonely Hearts Club Band.

BOBBITT

Greet Lorena Bobbitt, gator,
Outraged penile amputator
Who, like an avenging Venus,
Bobbitted her husband's penis.

ELVIS

Elvis Presley, alligator,
Graceland's pelvic oscillator,
Long ago, while young and slender,
Wowed his fans with "Love Me Tender."

AMAZING GRACE

Marion Barry, alligator,
Prodigal administrator,
Got the voters' benediction
By parading his conviction.
Born again and running free,
Barry's mayor of D.C.!

ALEXANDER

Alexander Alligator
Ordered candied sweet potater.
When the man was slow to cater,
Alexander ate the waiter.

THE BIRTH OF VENUS

Aphrodite, alligator,
Seeking to ingratiate her
Self with Botticelli, painter,
Posed as Beauty's newborn queen:
Venus Anadyomene.

LOU

Lou, a lissome alligator,
Sidesteps all attempts to mate her,
Saying, "I'd regret it, later!"
All the other gators hate her.

GONE WITH THE WIND

Rhett and Scarlett, alligators,
Volatile cohabitators,
Gorged each night on candied yam
Till Rhett didn't give a damn.

RENÉ DESCARTES

"I think, therefore I am an alligator."
Concluded René Descartes, cogitator.

ABOUT THE AUTHOR

When not fishing in Louisiana, NOËL MILLER lives in Washington, D.C., with her husband of thirty-one years. They have three grown children. This is her first book.